# the pain behind the Smile

### ANGELA FOXWORTH

Copyright © 2020 Angela Foxworth.

All rights reserved. No part of this publication may be re- produced, distributed, or transmitted in any form or by any means, including photocopying, recording, or other electronic or mechanical methods, without the prior written permission of the publisher, except in the case of brief quotations embodied in critical reviews and certain other noncommercial uses permitted by copyright law. For per- mission requests, write to the publisher, addressed "Attention: Permissions Coordinator," at the address below.

Author: Angela Foxworth

afox2440@yahoo.com

Publisher: Jesus, Coffee, and Prayer Christian

400 West Peachtree Rd. NW, STE 4-5055, Atlanta, GA 30308

www.jesuscoffeeandprayer.com

jesuscoffeeandprayer@gmail.com

Chief Editor: Jesus, Coffee, and Prayer Christian Publishing House

Cover/Layout/Design: Eswari Kamireddy

ISBN 978-1-952273-02-5

# Contents

Foreword ....................................................................... v

Acknowledgements ........................................................ ix

Preface ........................................................................ xv

Chapter One .................................................................. 1

Chapter Two .................................................................. 5

Chapter Three ................................................................ 9

Chapter Four ................................................................ 13

Chapter Five ................................................................ 19

Chapter Six .................................................................. 25

Chapter Seven .............................................................. 29

Chapter Eight ............................................................... 33

Chapter Nine ................................................................ 41

Chapter Ten .................................................................. 45

Chapter Eleven ............................................................. 49

Chapter Twelve ............................................................. 55

Chapter Thirteen ........................................................... 59

Chapter Fourteen .......................................................... 63

Chapter Fifteen ............................................................. 67

Chapter Sixteen ............................................................ 71

Chapter Seventeen ........................................................ 73

About the Author .......................................................... 77

# *Foreword*

### From Sean Wyman

As I stood in the Microsoft Store in Atlanta, Georgia I knew God had brought me here for a purpose. A beautiful woman with a dynamic personality and amazing smile was interviewing new authors and I was immediately engaged by her energy. I had no idea who she was or the story that was hiding inside of her, but I felt an immediate call to meet her.

I introduced myself and explained that I was a new author. I shared a glimpse into my story and the book I had written. She told me her name was Angela Foxworth and she was a host on a Gospel Radio Network who was here today interviewing new authors. She interviewed me on the spot and we had an immediate connection. From that day forward, God had a plan for Angela, and I thank him every day for using me to help her discover it.

Angela opened the door for me to have my own radio show and it was great learning from her amazing experience. What was even more amazing was when she called me and affirmed that my book had a divine purpose. She shared with me how it had inspired her to write a book and tell her story.

Understanding how powerful a story can be when told the right way, I had the honor of reading this story in its raw form and was so moved by the story Angela told. Then the greatest honor that can be asked of someone was afforded to me to write the foreword for Angela's book. If I am being completely honest I was floored. I had never been asked to do something so special and sentimental.

*There are millions of people in the world today who face trauma from adverse childhood experiences and never deal with it. Although trauma is only intended to last for a moment it ends up capturing a lot of people for their entire lifetime. As someone who has personally faced adverse experiences in my life, I can tell you if you are reading this book there is something inside waiting to impact you. –Angela Foxworth*

What is unique about Angela is the beauty that comes from sharing her adverse experiences in this book. That beauty is called love. She found the love within herself and realized she needed to share her story to serve others.

Through her transparency she has been able to release things that held onto her for many years as it has for so many others. Now Angela has confronted her past and she is going to impact others who have faced adversity in their life but have not had the courage up to this point to face it.

People who go through trauma face denial, regret, anger, misery, and anxiety. Most never truly heal from their pain. Instead fear, self-doubt, and manipulation take control of them mentally, physically, and spiritually. This book is an amazing journey of how Angela took the DRAMA in her life and turned all of her tests into testimonial attributes that have given her the strength, courage, and motivation to become the incredible woman she is today.

Read this book and discover how you can relate to the challenges and adverse experiences Angela faced then apply the lessons from her story and use them to find your voice. There are victims, survivors, and winners in life. Angela is a winner who has written a book that will impact, educate, and enable you to win back your life no matter what you have faced and encourage you to move forward.

-Sean Wyman
@successwithseanwyman
#keepmovingforward

# Acknowledgements

To my husband Stephen. We have gone through so much. We have had to overcome some huge obstacles. It has not been easy supporting me as this opportunity has turned our world upside down. We have talked about calling it quits several times. But, I am so grateful and thankful that you have decided to not only stay in the game with me, but help me with all of the things that I need. We have grown to be great friends and I am blessed to go on this journey with you. I don't know where we will end up. We both have learned to live and enjoy in the moment! I love you always. I am so blessed to share this life with you.

To my daughter Alicia, no matter what your struggles are you have the strength to keep going.
To my business partner and friend Angela Lewis thank you for pushing me into my destiny and continuing to challenge me. I will never forget it.

To my mentor and friend Sean Wyman, thank you for the success movement process. Your transparency encouragement and selflessness are the reasons why I push myself to write this book.
To my friend Erica Mosley thank you for your benevolence during the most difficult times in my life.

To my soulmate friend Tesha Goss Clayton, thank you for always supporting me and for making me truly feel like myself. Our years of friendship have been like fine wine, they just get better and better as the time goes on.
To my friend Patty Bato, you have been a part of my life since the beginning and I will always treasure our friendship

To my guardian angel Greta Samuels, thank you for always being there. I am so blessed to know you and thankful for our amazing friendship that has transcended time.

To my family and friends, support is necessary when you are trying to follow a dream. I appreciate each and every person in my life that has helped me in reaching my destiny.

# Preface

At this point, I began to feel uncomfortable. I had never hung around this crowd before, and his reputation was really bad. There was an extremely long silence as he took the gun joystick and continued to aim for the ducks.

Finally, he broke the silence by saying,

"You know you're not leaving until you give me what I want?" I tried to act like I did not hear him. I chuckled nervously because in mind I could not believe he was saying this. I did not know him. Never had a conversation with him…not once; yet he was threatening me to have sex with him.

He then turned to me and looked me in my eye and repeated,

"I'm serious, and you are not leaving here until you give me what I want." I was panicked at that point! How did I end up here? I was just trying to help a friend! I don't know any of these guys. And why would Tyrell do this to me? I hated this guy. He is disgusting and although, I had been promiscuous, I would not let him touch me with a 10-foot pole!

# The Pain Behind The Smile

He would have to rape me before I ever laid down with him! And that is exactly what he did!

> She's been through hell and came out, an angel. You didn't break her, darling. You don't own that kind of power.
>
> BMM Poetry

# Chapter One

There are times in your life when storms are going to come your way and overcoming those storms is what defines you. Some experience trials early in life, for others it may take a long time. But either way, the struggle is to move past the storm. The first horrible incident of my childhood took place when I was six years old and was physically abused by my great aunt. The reason for which we got beat was so minuscule, but the result of what transpired has lasted a lifetime. My cousin and I were playing on our carport at home. We were using one of those green water hoses. Every house on the block had one back then. We would drink out of them, wash the cars with them and water the grass with them. But on this particular day my cousin and I were being mischievous and decided to use it for a more recreational purpose. So, we sprayed each other down with water just playing around like kids often do. My aunt who was just starting out as an attorney came home and was livid at what she saw. We had turned over our play table set, water filled the carport and our clothes were completely soaked. She yelled at us and said she was going to beat us for what we did. We always kept a spare piece of green water hose that we used to jump rope with in the backyard. The hose was about 2 inches thick. My aunt cut the tip of the hose by putting slits in it. Once she was done it looked like a cat and nine tails at the end of it.

She made us both take off our clothes and one by one whipped our backs, arms and our legs. The whips tore into our flesh and began to bleed. The pain was unbearable!!! There were no words to describe the agony and torment you feel when your flesh is being torn apart. The only way I can describe it, is like knives stabbing you constantly. You cry out, but nothing stops the pain. We screamed and cried so loud. I was surprised our neighbors could not hear us. After the last whip, which seemed like an eternity, she ran our bath water and added alcohol to it and made us get in the water with our bloody, broken bodies. The pain was excruciating, and the tub filled with blood. During those years my mom was a single mom and lived with my great aunt to save money. My mom was furious when she got home! She could not believe my aunt had beaten us like that. I was told not to say a word. My mom put ointment on my entire body.

She laid me down until I went to sleep. The next day I went to school. I wore jeans and a wool top. I managed to be discreet and I did not breathe a word for fear I would get beaten again. But during lunch my first- grade teacher saw the blood and the pus seep through my jeans and she asked me to come over. She examined me and asked me what happened. I was hesitant at first, but once she had me turn around, she insisted on me telling her what happened. I broke down and told her. I was angry. Even at 6 years old I knew it was unfair to be abused like that. As much as I was afraid, I wanted her to be exposed more than anything. The next day there was an HRS worker at our house. HRS is the state's children service that investigates child abuse. She asked a lot of questions then asked my aunt what she used to beat us. At first my aunt lied about what she beat us with. She pulled out a thin, clear, plastic, rope-like object that would never be able to do the damage of what she had really used. In my desperation for her to get in trouble, I defiantly, ran into the room to show them exactly what it was she used. To my surprise they wrote down a few words and began to leave. I was so disappointed. I felt like there was no point in me attempting to expose her because HRS basically just gave her a warning. However, after some time had passed, I was glad she was exposed because she knew she would not be able to do it again and she didn't. It took 6 months for my scars to heal. However, the mental scars still remain today. I think there will always be residue in your life when tragedy happens. There are times in your life when storms are going to come your way and overcoming those storms is what defines you. Some experience trials early in life, for others it may take a long time. But either way, the struggle is to move past the storm.

    Yet still, I smiled.

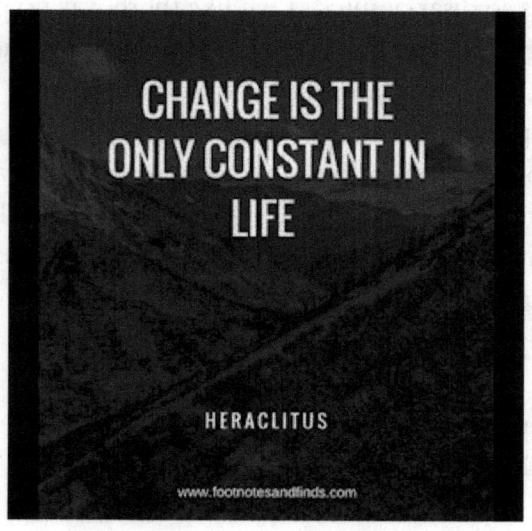

# Chapter Two

After the abuse incident, things were quite different from that point on. My aunt finally got a place of her own, and so did my mom. We lived in a nice area, and I had a normal childhood. It was just me, my mom and my baby brother. I was one of the few black kids in my neighborhood, but I always had great friends. All of us were very close. I was athletic and could sing. I joined the chorus. We were exposed to a lot of cultures, and our education was advanced; although, we were in an elementary school. But times were tough for my mom financially as a single parent, and eventually, my mother moved from our predominately white area into what you would probably call the hood.

Being a single mother, she had to make so many sacrifices and so much to do to make ends meet, and I can only imagine it must not have always been easy for her. I was now 10-years-old and in the fifth grade. It's funny how being in a predominately white area the schools are much more advanced. I was always an average student of A's, B's and C's. But at the predominantly black school I excelled beyond measure and was a straight A student. You can imagine though, after five years of being around nothing but white people I sounded very foreign when I went to the fifth-grade school with all black students. Top that off with being slightly chubby to the point my mother was embarrassed about me and therefore did not put a lot of stock in my dress code. So, I wore bellbottoms when they were not popular. I had a closet of about six outfits that I had to interchange to maximize my use of them. And, to add insult to injury, I had a short haircut because of a Jerry curl my mother put in my hair unnecessarily which made it all fall out!!! So, whether I intended to or not, I was going to be popular no matter what, and not in a good way!!! The kids in my school were hip and trendy. They knew all the latest lingo in the urban dictionary. They were up on all the latest fashions trends and wore the best brands that welfare could buy. They could recite all the scenes of the most popular urban television shows and they could also go out and party at the hottest teen spots around town. None of those things existed in my world. Because I was extremely sheltered. My life was television, fantasy imaginations, and dreaming that I was somewhere different longing for a different life.

This kind of school did take some getting used to. I remember the first time I got punched by a boy named Josh as I began to transition to the new school. As far back as I can remember, I hated bullies. I've always felt the need to take up for people who could not take up for themselves. So, of course, my first day having to ride the bus was a challenge because no sooner than I opened my mouth to say *'hello'*, James came over to me to eject something smart out of his lips.

He immediately began laughing with the people on the bus

stop saying, "Who is this girl? Look at what she is wearing and listen to how she talks. She sounds stupid." He went on and on. So, in my normal sarcastic fashion, I fired back. "Who sounds stupid? The girl who speaks proper because she enunciates her words due to being educated or the boy who is just ignorant?"

It must have struck a nerve because instantly I felt a powerful blow to the right side of my face nevertheless, I was and still am a fighter. I realized, even back then, it was just how I was built. I tried my hardest to hit him back, and I did manage to connect a couple of good punches. Unfortunately, he had delivered a far more impactful blow. Everyone all around us seemed to be in shock, but they continued to laugh among each other. I sat by myself alone on the bus as stranger not knowing anyone. I felt like I was in a very strange land so different from the environment and neighborhood I grew up in. It was more like a culture shock where every day we would hang out after school and play with each other sharing our crayons and markers, running around laughing and playing and just loving each other.

As I look back and thought about that incident, I realized that I was probably always going to be different and stand out. That would mean some very lonely days would be ahead of me.

Ironically, I have realized that being different has made me not only extremely stronger and able to stand on my own, but a force to be reckoned with. I was a chubby black girl that had grown up around a white majority with no fashion sense and was not very attractive. This taught me not to care or be concerned with what anyone thought of me.

Yet still, I smiled.

> You have to fight through some bad days to earn the best days of your life.

# Chapter Three

After the incident with James, things seemed to get better. What I realized is when you take up for yourself, and you don't back down even if you lose a fight, people respect the fight in you. James and I even became very good friends. And I begin to make a lot of friends. I was very well liked and popular even though I was not considered "the norm."

People seem to overlook the fact that I could not dress and didn't have the best of everything, but they loved my smile and my personality. My teachers would always call me "mouth almighty" and "mighty mouth!"

I guess you can say I was always destined to be a talk show host since I got in trouble for talking all the time. Like anything in life, things can be going very well and then you hit a rough patch. Mine began in the form of my first official bully! Virginia Green was her name.

Virginia Green was her name. She was a chocolate girl that was about 6-feet tall in the sixth grade. Everyone was scared of her, and she took quite advantage of it. My mission that I had no choice but to except was to bring her a kosher dill pickle every day. Now, how I was going to achieve this task was equally challenging.

My mother made my lunch every day, so I never had lunch money. I had to come up with $.50 per day to purchase a kosher dill pickle. There was a store house in the beautiful home district of Paradise Park. It is where all the kids would go for any snacks they wanted. You had your choice of pickles and chips, candies and chocolates and ice cream and Honey drippers. I was faced with the dilemma of not only having to come up with the money to purchase these delectable items, but also getting to the store house with enough time to be on time for school. So not only was I going to have to come up with the money but also the time to get to the storehouse before going to school. It was not on my way home. The storehouse was not in the direction of my home. But, with any task I was given, I worked very hard to find a solution. At the time I lived with my grandparents, and my grandfather drank a lot. He also made very good money as a fisherman but didn't use a lot of his money to invest. He had empty Wild Turkey bottles that he would fill with pennies. When I was a kid, I thought it was millions of dollars because he had over 20 or 30 bottles filled. Every day for months I would bring one pickle a day to Virginia, and she was completely content with that. I managed to stay on her good side for most of the year.

Then one night, devastation took place. My granddaddy realized I had been taking pennies out of his jars. He said I was no longer allowed to go into his Wild Turkey bottles to get pennies.

I was panicked the entire night. I could not sleep because I knew what my fate would be if I walked into that classroom without Felicia's Kosher deal pickle. I begged my granddaddy to reconsider and was answered with an emphatic no!

Needless to say, I got to school without the pickle, and Virginia let me know that immediately after school at 3 o'clock, she was going to beat me down. Her exact words. As the day approached, my heart raced faster and faster. I could not concentrate on anything but the fact that I was going to get beat down by Virginia! And it didn't help that multiple people in school that were afraid of her kept reminding me about the 3 o'clock deadline. So 3 o'clock approached and my plan was to go home super-fast before Virginia could get me. My girlfriend Malesha Williams, was by my side the entire time and our little buddy Robbie. They briskly began to walk home with me supporting me as I tried to get away from Virginia. But it was no use Virginia had practically the entire gang from school behind her, and she began to catch up with me. The closer she got, the more panicked I became. Then I felt her hand pressed against my shoulder and my fear turned into panicked rage. I just began to whale my arms hitting her repeatedly out of fear and then picked her up and slammed her on the ground. People were screaming and chanting all around us, older teenagers were calling me Rick Flair. She got a few hits in but ultimately, I beat her down!

The next day when we arrived it was all over the school how I beat Virginia Green. After that, I never heard a peep from her and I finished out my school year unscathed. Another life lesson that I learned is when you take up for yourself if nothing else, people will respect you.

Yet still, I smiled.

# The Pain Behind The Smile

# Chapter Four

The following years were great! I was involved in many activities from cheerleading to volleyball to chorus and running track. Being in a strict household, it was my only outlet. I took full advantage of it. After my six-grade year and leaving the school as the legend that beat up Virginia Green, we moved back to the predominately white neighborhood I came from. Most of my elementary school friends were still attending the school so going back to my old neighborhood was great.

Our schools were separated by junior high and high school. Seventh, eighth and ninth grades were junior high and tenth, eleventh and twelfth were considered high school. Transitioning from the ninth grade to the tenth grade was a huge shift in my life. I left ninth grade with a lot of awards for all of the auxiliaries I was in and with most school spirit. I decided to keep myself busy for that summer. I would go to summer school and take classes that could get me ahead for my high school year. Seemed like a great idea at the time I just never knew it would change my life forever.

As you know, sex is always a very important topic in high school. Hormones are all over the place and boys want to show that they can conquer as many girls as possible. I was a huge tease. Because of my extensive vocabulary, I could talk a great game but whenever it got down to doing it; no way Jose. It's funny how things turned out. And in junior high there was a click of about seven of us girls that were very good friends. We made a pact to tell each other when we would lose our virginity. Believe it or not, I was picked to be first. This pact started in the seventh grade. Out of everyone I was next to the last to lose my virginity.

Looking back on what took place, I really wish I had the strength not to give into peer pressure. But of course, hindsight is 20/20. It all began the summer I was in school. Again, I was transitioning to my sophomore year and I decided to take extra classes to get ahead. I just did not want to spend my summer all cooped up in the house. I did not realize how much fun summer school was. All of the rebellious students attended because they did not pass the regular school year. As a result, everyone that made school fun was in summer school! I also got the opportunity to make friends with people I normally wouldn't have.

Then I met Ethan. He was very attractive!! Every girl wanted him to be with him. He had a reputation for the ladies. And he knew it. His confidence was just as attractive as he was. We began to talk and laugh because we had a class together. I never thought of our relationship as being anything other than strictly friends. You see I was the chubby girl that usually hooked up my guy friends with my pretty girlfriends. I was never the girl they wanted to date. I was just cool, and I was OK with that. I mean, I had a few little boy friends along the way, but I was always attracted to older boys. I believe it was because my dad was not in my life. But Ethan was mature and therefore very alluring. One day after school, he asked did I want a ride home. I declined but he insisted. My mom was not at home in the afternoons, which caused me to be very leery about letting people in the house when she was not there. My mom always found a way of finding out if I had done something wrong and the consequences were deadly. But there was just something so irresistible about Ethan and literally he would not take no for an answer. Once he dropped me off, he walked me to my door and kissed me. It was an amazing kiss and I could not believe how my entire body responded. I let him in and we made out, but when the time came for me to go all the way I asked him to stop. He tried a few times after that and I still said no. It frustrated him and therefore he told me if I became known in school as a big tease no guy would ever date me. Normally that type of response would not phase me, but he was a junior and this was going to be my first year at this school, so I began to worry about my overall reputation. Peer pressure crept in.

Now that I am older of course I know better. However, back then I let him convince me that what he was saying would be the case. So, the following day I decided to let him take me home again and I lost my innocence in my mother's bedroom. As soon as it was over, he left and never even talked to me after that.

I felt horrible because it was my first time and I really did not know what to do or what to expect. Fifteen years old and now I was no longer a virgin. The rejection after getting what he wanted affected me in many ways.

After that incident, I suddenly began to get propositioned by guys in school. I never understood why, but again I realized later that he had bragged to so many guys about being with me. I was never quite the same after that.

    Yet still, I smiled.

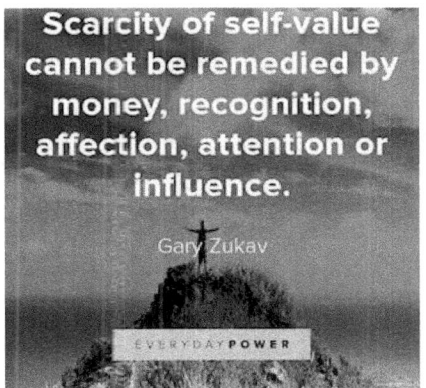

# Chapter Five

My life dramatically changed from this point on going forward. I began to get propositioned by some of the best-looking guys in high school and it was all due to one rumor they heard about me no longer being a virgin. Really?? It was Ethan's big mouth!

Growing up for me was a little more challenging because I was the oldest out of two brothers. My parents divorced when I was two years old, and each one of them had a son six years after my birth. My dad's love and desire to have a son was very apparent in his absenteeism in my life. My mother loved her baby boy, and of course, typically the babies are spoiled and get all the attention and he got just that. I've never resented either one of my brothers because I love them dearly. I just never felt significant to anybody…not my mother nor my father. In retrospection, this new-found attention I was receiving was new to me, and it was definitely tempting. And then my mother made another big move.

This was a decision to save money so that she could eventually buy a house and get her finances under control.

She decided to move in with her best friend across the river. Now this neighborhood was not the hood, but it was predominantly black. I was going to have to take two modes of public transportation every day in order to get home because she still wanted me to stay at schools that provided the best education. There was only one problem with this move. My mother's best friend's son. His name was Hamp Jackson. Hamp was a superstar football player who was awarded a full scholarship to college.

Everything about him caught my eye. He was 6'4," muscular tone, muscular body, and in great shape. The move took place a couple of months before the summer break. He would be leaving for college at the end of the summer. I had known him since I was a little girl.

Before this move, we only had one uncomfortable encounter, where he inappropriately propositioned me. I said no, so nothing ever happened. That was three years before this move, and of course, neither one of our parents knew anything about it. Life for us was always like that. As far back as I can remember when bad things happened in my family that needed to be addressed, we would never speak on it. We just acted like it never took place.

Denial.

So, once that incident happened, I just stopped thinking about it and put it to the back of my mind.

But now three years later we are about to begin living together. And I am no longer a virgin anymore. I was so nervous. Moving day finally arrived, and we had decided to move over the weekend so that we could be in place by that Monday. When we finally came face to face, he was very nice and made re-introducing ourselves very comfortable. We spent the whole day transferring rooms, making things fit and putting our things together. It ended up being an extremely productive day. It was great! My guard was down, and I began to look forward to moving in. So that night after a grueling day of moving all of us; my mom, her best friend, me and Hamp all decided to just sit down and relax. Once my mom and her best friend went to sleep Hamp came to me and said,

"Are you ready for tomorrow?"

I knew exactly what he was talking about by the way he said it. He wanted to finish what we started three years before. I said yes nervously, but deep down I was terrified even though I had already lost my virginity. And although I was super nervous, I slept great that night from the fatigue of moving.

It was around 7 o'clock in the morning, and I heard my mom and her best friend getting ready to leave for work. I began to shake badly. I tried to act like I was in a deep sleep. I heard the door close, and the car leave. About 10 minutes went by and nothing. About 15 more went by still nothing. At that moment, I felt like he had changed his mind and relief came all over me. As soon as I was relaxed and began to fall asleep again, I felt a hand rub my leg. Immediately my nerves were shot again. For a moment, I had a brief conversation with myself wondering why I was so scared because it was not like back when I when I was younger- this was three years later. The reasoning in my head soon began to disappear as he bent down to kiss me.

I began to feel things I never realized a woman could feel. I'd want to compare my first experience with this one and realized there was no comparison. Everything about it!

It was addicted.

The second time was the *charm* and led to a lifestyle of promiscuity.

The attention became addictive. I had never felt this wanted in my entire life. I rarely dealt with high school boys, I preferred college and up. A few were older men. I was never really into young guys. They seemed silly and immature. Probably felt that way because of my daddy issues. I had no intentions of stopping what I was doing though because it felt so good to be desired, but life has a way of putting things in perspective for you even when you don't. Sin entangles

Yet still, I smiled.

*"Sometimes our desires in life feel good but are not always good for us. God knows what's best. If you don't put an end to the things that He knows are not good, He will. That is the greatest love he has for us."*

— A. Fox

# Chapter Six

At this particular time, summer proved to be very adventurous. That summer I had more lovers than I could count, and my final fling was with a 35-year-old man. He was attractive, charismatic and passionate. I had fallen completely in love with him, or so I thought, as much as you can be in love at 15-years-old.

I remember sitting in class half paying attention just dreaming about our moments together. As soon as that final bell would ring at school, I remember jumping on both of my buses in anticipation of seeing him. He was one of my neighbors, and when I would get home, I would throw my books down and go to his house knowing I had a few hours to spend with him before my mom got home. It still puzzles me to this day how everything came to an end.

The incident that changed everything took place one Saturday night at the fair. It took me forever to beg my mother and convince her to let me go to Midnight Madness! For a teenager, that was the place to be.

You ride all the rides you want for $10 from midnight to

five in the morning. Anybody who was anybody was at this event. After a solid two weeks of begging my mother, she finally decided to let me, go! And to add the icing to the cake, she was letting me go with Hamp! So of course, once we left the house that evening, he had other plans that took place before the fair. We stopped by one of his friend's house for more promiscuous activities, with him and his friend, but not at the same time.

Out of peer pressure, I drank beer too. I didn't even like the taste of it. I did it anyway. After that stop, we proceeded to a best friend's house party for more shenanigans before the fair.

There I flirted with my friends older brother. We had a brief moment of flirtatious kissing. We laughed, danced and then finally headed to the fair. We had a great time riding all the rides, eating our fair share of junk food and enjoying our friends.

It was almost like the shenanigans before the fair didn't even take place. When it was all said and done, we went home completely drained.

Yet still, I smiled.

If you're wrong. Own up to what you didn't do right. That's how you learn and earn respect.

# Chapter Seven

The weekend following the fair was a typical one. Hamp's girlfriend came to visit, so we didn't have any intimate time. Oh, I guess I did not mention that earlier.

Despite our shenanigans, he had a girlfriend. It did not matter anyway because I was so smitten with Ben, my 35-year-old lover that lived around the corner. I wasn't missing Hamp at all. Ben made me feel like the most beautiful girl in the world. My entire adolescents was filled with - you're too fat and boyish.

Daddy issues~ some would call it.

When you don't have a father who wants to spend time with you, it is easier to be manipulated~ believing that you are beautiful~ even if they are just using you.

As I grew older, I have come to grips that our relationship was completely inappropriate; but at the time age just did not matter to me. He seemed to enjoy every curve I had. In his world, it was an asset not a liability. He embraced my athletic side. He did not think of me as boyish. He said it added value to our relationship. of the sexual explorations I experienced with him. Oddly enough he was also like a father figure to me. He would give me real life advice on so many things and genuinely was an awesome person to talk to. My maturity level was always greater than my age because I had to grow up quickly.

The conversations between Ben and I were very relatable. And of course, at age 15, I had a coke bottle figure like Beyoncé He loved my firm yet very soft body. On that Saturday, like most I would sneak over to his house for our one on one time.

The next day of course, was Sunday and our typical morning consisted of getting up early to be at Sunday school at church. Growing up, my mother never really went to church but when we moved in with her best friend who was an avid churchgoer, she felt obligated to go. Surprisingly, enough she did get her calling and began to speak at certain events at church.

Then she became a Sunday school teacher for the youth. I have always had the talent to sing but had complete anxiety when it came to execute it. My mother forced me to be the lead soprano in our youth choir. When I arrived at church, I would sit in the back with my Sunday school teacher while my mother taught the pre-teens.

Typically, we would all join each other to sit in the congregation once Sunday school had ended. This particular Sunday I decided to sit with a girlfriend. We were talking about all the things I did over the weekend. My Friend looked at my neck and said, "Did you know you had a hickey on your neck?" I explained that I did not know. I had forgotten that part of the weekend. When I got up and went to the bathroom and looked in the mirror, sure enough there was a big hickey on the right side of my neck completely visible for anybody to see. My only prayer at that moment was to get through Sunday school and church long enough to make it home and hide my neck.

But, remember I told you earlier how one small thing can shift your entire world? When church was over with we began exiting the sanctuary. In my heart of hearts, I had gotten away *'scott free'* without my mother seeing my neck. Suddenly, I hear this loud voice roar from across the street!

"Come here Angela!"

As I begin to walk across the street, I began sweating profusely walking in what appeared to be in slow motion. It felt like I was walking the *Green Mile*. It was my mother. No sooner than I reached her, she surveyed the side of my neck. Tilting my head sideways, she immediately asked me, "What is that on your neck?!" At that moment my life froze. The realization of what was about to take place seemed catastrophic.

Yet still, I smiled.

## Rape

R was my reaction,
I laid there very still,
My thoughts were simply nothing,
To him this was a drill.

A is for advantage,
That's what he thought of me
Or maybe even less, who knows.
How could I let this be?

P is for pathetic,
It's how I feel inside.
Behind the pain and bruises, too
Is where I have to hide.

E is just for everything,
I let him take it all.
I couldn't fight him off of me,
Thanks to alcohol.

Shayler Caruth

# Chapter Eight

With a lump forming in my throat, I managed to swallow a gulp of saliva.

"Nothing mama!"

I knew that was not going to work. She placed her forefinger and thumb against my chin turning my head slightly sideways to get a clearer view and of course, there it was. Gritting her teeth, she told me to get in the car, and the rest was a blur after that.

Of what I do remember? She made like she worked for the FBI and interrogated me relentlessly about my virginity. And wouldn't you know it, I continued to lie. But like a senior, special FBI agent in charge she was adamant about getting her answers and she would not give up! She was determined to know where I got the hickey from and whether or not I was still a virgin.

Here is the irony of all of this. The guy that gave me the hickey was not the guy I lost my virginity to and the guy I was having sex with was not the guy I lost my virginity to! Yes, shaking your head, right? Leave it to me to create such havoc in my own life especially after being worn down and yelled at about it daily. Then one day, my mom decided to use her "jokers wildcard." She took me to the doctor to confirm if I had been sexually active. I was panic stricken and knew I was going to go down fast like the Titanic! I knew it was a do or die moment. So, I spilled the beans and told her everything even about the 35-year-old man! I was caught- RED handed.

It was horrible!!

I had never seen my mom so disappointed in me and so angry. Our irresponsible behavior drove a wedge between our moms. Hank and I never spoke again. And I don't even know what happened to my 35-year-old lover.

My mom and I moved out and back to the neighborhood we had come from. She was still very livid with me, but slowly began to communicate again. Truthfully, there was never any real communication between us anyway. At that time in my life, I looked at my mom as more of a dictator than a parent. There was never any warm and fuzzy mother and daughter moments. I feared her greatly. But at least for now she was more tolerable. I still attended the same school and worked hard to leave all men alone. Because of the devastating result of what took place, I felt an enormous amount of guilt. My mom was not talking to her best friend at all.

I blamed myself.

Even though, my partner was a grown man and I was a child, I still felt extremely responsible for my part.

### The Change

I **prayed** every day that everyone would forgive me, and

I could get a do-over, but life just does not work that way. *Eventually, you reap what you sow,* and I was reaping severely. This occurred a few months after we moved back to the old neighborhood. After this entire incident I changed my surroundings, the people I hung around and the boys/men I associated with. I wanted to be someone new.

It was the day before the last day of school and at that time I was rolling with an entirely new crew. The guy I liked was considered a nerd and my new girlfriend Talia was a young lady that had been bullied the previous year. She eventually came in to her own and began to be the beautiful swan princess that she always wanted to be.

We had so much fun together, and our new boyfriends were a part of the same click. Her boyfriend was Amon, and my boyfriend was Kenneth. The rest of the crew consisted of Roger, Ben, and Paul. We hung out with all of them, but it was just good clean fun. Just what I needed at that time, but everything was about to change.

School was about to end and Talia and I were double dutching in the gym. We were talking about the guys when she mentioned she had not heard from Answar. She was worried but decided she would just speak with him later. About an hour went by, and she still had not heard from him. She got a phone call and was told he was at an apartment nearby. She was determined to find him. She asked if I would come with her and I emphatically said no. I had been walking a tightrope with my mom, and I refused to get into any more trouble. I was forbidden to go anywhere but home. But Talia begged and begged, and I finally gave in to the temptation.

The apartment was in walking distance of the school. It was roughly about a 20 minute walk. When we arrived at the complex, I recognized the area. It was a rough part of town. The school rebels and criminals were known to live there, and that crowd was not the crowd I hung around. I knew of them because of their bad reputation, but I did not know any of them personally. I began to feel a little anxious. I was already nervous about going, but once I realized it was kind of a bad neighborhood, I felt even worse. But she found the exact apartment, and I did not want to let her go in by herself. She knocked on the door when we arrived, and some guy opened the door. He looked like a gang member, and he told us to come in.

Upon entering the apartment, we were immediately standing in the living room. The kitchen was straight ahead, and the dining room sat off to your direct right. At the kitchen table, sat two guys cleaning guns, and stacked up against the wall on the kitchen counter were large amounts of white blocks wrapped in plastic saran wrap.

Back then I had no idea what it was, but knowing what I know now, it was cocaine. There were more guns in the corner of another room and three guys playing a video game in the spare bedroom as we continued to walk further in. We stood in the middle of the desolate looking living room for what seemed like an eternity which was really for only about 3 minutes. Abruptly, one of the guys told Talia to follow him and that Answar was in the room off to the right. She walked down this bleak hallway which I lost sight of her.

Now I'm totally alone in this place with a bunch of criminals. At this point, I was terrified to say the least. Suddenly, the door to the left opened and a familiar face popped out. Unfortunately, it was not a welcoming face.

The guy was Tyrell, a big time gang member and drug dealer at our school. I NEVER hung out with him, let alone had any dealings with him at all. He was fat, grimy looking, and very intimidating. I knew of him because his girlfriend worked with me at Womack's Hamburgers. She was sixteen years old and pregnant. There were all kinds of rumors about her. She was known to be a very promiscuous girl that had given a few guys an STD. She was also rumored to have had multiple abortions. And they were both rumored for having a volatile relationship and constant fist fights.

Consequently, to see him did not make me feel any more comfortable. His eyes looked directly at me and signaled for me to come to the room he was in. I hesitated but he strongly insisted. When I stepped inside of the room, to my surprise it was a normal bedroom. He was sitting on the bed and playing the Nintendo game Duck Hunt.

At this point, my 'Spidey senses' began to feel dangerously uncomfortable. As I have stated before, I had never hung around this type of crowd before and his bad reputation really surpassed him. There was an extremely long silence as he took the gun's joystick and continued to aim for the ducks.

Finally, he broke his silence.

"You know you're not leaving until you give me some, right?" I tried to act like I did not hear him. I chuckled nervously because in my mind I could not believe what my ears were hearing what he was saying. I did not know him. Never even had a conversation with him. And now standing before him before him, he was threatening to have sex with me? He then turned to me and looked me directly into my eyes.

"I'm serious. You are not leaving here until you give me some!" I quickly began to panic at this point. How did I end up here?! I was just trying to help a friend! I don't know any of these guys. And why would Tyrell do this to me? I hate this fat, ugly looking guy. He is disgusting and as promiscuous as I have been, I would not let him touch me with a 10-foot pole. He would have to rape me before I would ever lay down with him! And that is exactly what happened. He jumped up forcing my body down, ripping off my panties and penetrated me from behind.

The only way I could describe the moment was pain and death.

I was helpless.

I was just violated in the worse way, raped, degraded, and used like a piece of trash!

I was now an insignificant human being. Abused and discarded. I hated this man with all my being. If I had a knife or a gun I would have killed him. With every stroke I felt weaker and weaker and angrier and angrier. He did not even look at the fact that I was crying hysterically.

This gutless trash who had to take what he wanted with no regards for my life showed not one ounce of remorse.

A rapist! That is what he was. And when he finished, he pushed me from behind and queued the next guy to come in and do the same thing!

I was mortified.

By now I was being held down in a closet while one by one they each raped me…a total of five of them!

Now you would think that was enough. But to add insult to injury of an already volatile situation, the last two guys were my friends. Yes, my friends!

Remember the crew that I had grown close to? Ben and Paul were the last two guys to rape me! I could do nothing but lay there in total humiliation, shock, pain, and disgust. Of all of them, they were supposed to be my *friends*! They were supposed to look out for me like a sister! How could they not help me, protect me, save me?

I cried so much, I went physically numb. I could not even feel my tears anymore. When Paul got on top of me, I finally mustered up the word…*Why?* As a tear fell from the webs of my eyes. Like a monster, he pushed my head to the side and yelled, "Just shut up! Shut up!" I could see the tears forming in his eyes. I could sense he did not want to be there either. After he finished raping me, he lifted me up- letting me go.

"Run!"

And I did just that! I ran out of there as fast as I could. What the heck happened to Talia? I never found her. I finally made it home and ran bath water as hot as I could stand it. Upon sitting in the tub, I cried while scrubbing myself repeatedly until I almost rubbed my skin off. I wanted to just forget the atrocities that had just happened to me.

The aftermath was just the beginning.

Yet still, I smiled.

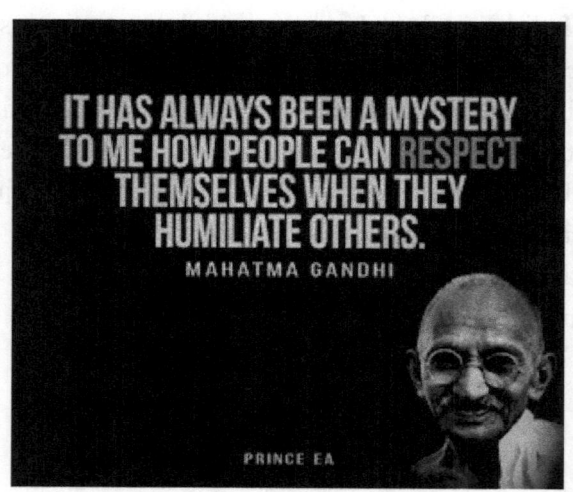

# Chapter Nine

I was numb all evening. I kept re-playing the events that took place a few hours earlier. My mother kept asking me what was wrong, and I told her I was just tired. I could not tell her. She would somehow find a way to make it my fault. I could not tell anyone.

I began to think about the law of reaping what you sow. I had slept with so many men. I was not careful and had become addicted to being wanted. A feeing I just did not grow up with. I had never felt significant to anyone. But when I had men not just young guys wanting to be with me, it made me feel special, wanted and needed.

So, in reality, I felt like I deserved what happened to me. It was bound to happen with the choices I had been making.

So, I told myself that to get through the night. I finally fell asleep.

The next day proved to be the worst day of my life. It was the last day of school. I dreaded going. I was very popular in school, sophomore class president to be more specific and therefore, everyone knew me. When I got to school, I tried to find Talia. She did not show up. But I did run into the crew, but instead of the normal banter and fun there was snickering and ridicule! What the world was going on?!! Ben and Paul were standing among them with no remorse! I thought to myself, how could anyone ridicule me and call me names after what those guys did to me? How insensitive can people be? It seemed like no matter where I walked or where I went some click was making comments at me. I felt so alone and isolated. I saw the head culprit of all of this, Tyrell. He and his crew were just standing there saying nothing. They acted as if none of it ever happened. I was so embarrassed!! I was so ready to leave the school. And still Talia was nowhere to be found. I began to blame her. If she had not convinced me to go with her then I would not have been ganged raped and my life would have been wonderful. But now, I am sitting here being accused of being a sleazy girl~ that everyone in the school knew about and had an opinion. When I finally ran into one of my true friends, she explained to me what was being said. Those lying guys said they ran a "train" on me and I sexed them all. I could not believe it! And why would anyone in this school believe those criminals? Why would anyone one trust what they said? It was the worst day of my life. I heard something from everyone no matter where I walked. Embarrassing and hurtful things were said all day long. I had to re-live that hurt all over again.

    Finally, the day ended, and I was headed home. I felt raped all over again.

    I went home defeated and abused. The only saving grace was that I had the entire summer to escape! My life was changed forever, and I will NEVER EVER feel the same about men ever again!

    Yet still, I smiled.

> Our prayers may be awkward. Our attempts may be feeble. But since the power of prayer is in the One who hears it and not in the one who says it, our prayers do make a difference.
>
> – Max Lucado

# Chapter Ten

There are special moments in your life that you know beyond a shadow of a doubt that God is real!

That summer proved to be the case for me. I stayed in most of the summer. I was like a caterpillar hanging upside down, spinning crazy in my mind as I began to transform into a silky shiny chrysalis, as God was keeping me protected. Then suddenly, he transformed my body, mind, and soul into a renewed creature that turned out to be a beautiful butterfly. I just wanted to put the whole incident behind me as if it never happened. I kept praying every day for a miracle to happen so that I would never have to go to that school or face those people ever again. And God answered those prayers.

Each day I had the same routine. I would get up in the morning and exercise by walking around outside by myself. I had no friends at that time as far as I was concerned. I did not speak to anyone the entire summer. I enjoyed my own company and loved spending time with my little brother. After everything that had transpired, I felt like that is what I should have been doing to begin with. Guilt would sometimes play on my emotions, causing me to feel like I had gotten what I deserved somehow. When those feelings would surface, I would just bury myself into television. That was my ultimate outlet. I was addicted to teen movies where the nerd girl gets the guy or inspirational movies like the karate kid. I'd also escape harsh realities by reading Harlequin romance novels all summer long fantasizing about a do over in my life, trying to erase all the bad decisions that I had made. Each day was like this for me throughout the entire summer. And then a concrete miracle took place.

There was about two weeks left before school was scheduled to start and I was receiving the information about what to expect for the upcoming school year. My mom came home early that day and told me she had something to tell me. I was nervous and did not know what to expect. All I knew was that I had not done anything to get in any kind of trouble.

Then it happened!

Our home had been ironically rezoned for re-districting and going forward I would have to start my junior year at an entirely new school!

My mom was kind of nervous, thinking that I would be upset leaving the school of people that I had known since kindergarten. Nevertheless, she had no idea what happened to me nor the mental cruelty I had endured. She had no clue how relieved I really was. Ecstatic was more like it!

**ptcv*I knew God was real and I mean really real,*** at that very moment because I had prayed and prayed for a miracle to happen. And it did. No longer will I have to face those people ever again in life. God is amazing! This blessing came in the form of a school redistricting that my mother was not even aware of! The peace of mind that came with this news was indescribable. I felt like I could breathe again. I jumped for joy and hugged my mom. She was so thankful as I began to get so excited about my new life starting at a new school! In the remaining two weeks of summer, I began to get information on my new school and classes and the school size and where my new bus stop would be. I had never been so happy in my entire life! I would think about the beginning of the summer as being in a cocoon which allowed me to gain so much change and reflection in my life. The metamorphosis that took place allowed me to become renewed and prepared me for the new beginning with new opportunities and a second chance to get my life right.

The morning I started my new journey. I was anxious and excited at the same time as I got ready to start my day. At this point in my life, I had endured so much.

Yet still, I smiled.

*"There is such a beauty in God answering prayers. However, just remember life is a set of trials, tests and testimonies. Never forget the blessing, but always look forward to the next journey. It never appears the way you expect it will."*

— A. Fox

# Chapter Eleven

The first day of school started and it was more than what I expected! The school was huge!

Seventh, eighth and ninth grade were on one side. Tenth, eleventh and twelfth grade was situated on the other side. It was the only school set up that way. No one knew who I was. I went from extremely popular to a big nobody and **I loved it**.

School was my outlet because my mother was very strict and did not allow me to hang out at my friends' homes or go to teen clubs. Hence, I was a very sheltered young lady.

Going to school was my form of entertainment and socialization. Oddly enough, I loved to learn; so I really felt at home at school. As I walked the halls on the first day, I felt alive. This was my do over and I was going to take full advantage of it. I was focused on education and work. I had no time for anything else, especially dating. I met some great people. There was a difference in the kind of people that attended this school.

The people I grew up with in elementary school and my

former high school were considered well-off. So, there was a certain air about the people that attended that school. They were great people, but they were perceived to be stuck up. But here at the new school, the people were more down to earth, and their parents were more working class as opposed to those of the upper middle class and the wealthy.

In other words, the people at my new school were more relatable. They understood my situation~ being raised by a single mother and money knowing that money did not grow on trees. With that being said, I met some great people and solid friends. I managed to get through most of the year without any relationships with the opposite sex. Somehow that changed with only three months left in the school year. For that reason, I had become so oblivious to guys and dating, I didn't realize when someone had genuinely liked me.

I was in the best shape of my life and since I was very focused, I decided I would try out for cheerleading. It was something I always wanted to do at my previous high school but I was told that I didn't fit in. I was more of an athletic type not the feminine type. Although, I was a cheerleader in the sixth grade and was very good at it. I had become determined in my mind I was going to try out no matter what. As I began try outs, I met more of the popular kids in school and of course cheerleaders who had been cheering since elementary school.

Everyone knew each other, and I officially became the new kid on the block. Similarly, this school was predominantly white. I would be one of the few minorities on the squad. The previous squad had one biracial beauty and one beautiful ebony princess who was leaving. She lived two complexes down from my apartment complex and took a liking to me. We grew into becoming very good friends.

She helped me with various dance routines as well as practices after school with no complaints. My cheerleading coach also took a liking to me and really thought I was special. She made me feel like a royal beauty...as if I could conquer anything. The encouragement she gave me was like an unyielding love with no regards to me being a thick girl.

I had never felt attractive in my life. My self-esteem began accelerating at an unsurpassed speed because growing up as I've stated before, my mother really made me feel like I was too big and not attractive enough for "girly" things. Trying out for the high school cheerleading team was something I had to not only prove to myself but also to those around me that doubted me. I knew I could do it. What I did not realize was how much positive attention I would gain as a cheerleader. By default, you get the pic of the best guys in school especially the athletes. I was never the typical prototype for what a beauty queen looked like, being of a large frame, short hair, black and rich-less. Sooner than later

I became very popular, very fast.

My first cousin had been attending that same school since the seventh grade. She told me that she was amazed at how I knew more people in less than one year then she knew in the four years she had been attending~ this time in a positive way. As we were soon approaching the last three months of school, I began to realize how I sparked the interest of the opposite sex. Despite this, I had definitely made up my mind that I did not want to date anyone. Little did I know this would change eventually.

In order to get ahead, I took summer classes. I wanted to take senior classes my junior year. This enabled me to take it easy my senior year. I was the only junior in an all senior contemporary history and law studies class. I loved both classes since they were extremely interactive, although we had a very strict teacher, Mrs. Yasmine. In my opinion, she looked every bit of 100 years old! Her voice was raspy, but she remained quite the dresser.

History has always been my favorite subject and I was always born with an inquisitive nature, so I fit right in with my class. I also loved public speaking. I've always felt very comfortable voicing my opinion and having open debates. There was nothing more for filling than speaking and disputing topics as it related to history and law studies.

On the other hand, there was a young man in my class who simply annoyed me, Mitchell. He was a 6'3" slender white young gentleman with sandy blond hair and chameleon eyes that changed from green to gray. He was the typical *All-American White guy*. He had a quiet confidence, or some would even say a cockiness. Mitchell often spoke his mind in class and was very opinionated. He was very sarcastic in his own right which caused us to often battle. His comments were so condescending and annoying. I always felt that he may have been racist. And every time he opened his big mouth I could not wait to shut him down with my Teflon opinion. Each interaction we encountered infuriated me, but he always seemed to be cool as a cucumber. He was friends with a guy name Steph that I thought was a great guy. I could not believe he was friends with this jerk! Steph would tell me all the time he's not so bad you just have to get used to him. In my mind I just wanted to put him in his racist place. We battled, so to speak, the entire year. The last three months of school were extremely conflict- ridden.

In the meantime, there was also a young athlete in my

homeroom class ~Roger. All the ladies wanted him because he was a top football player and a wrestler. He was a 6'5" bodybuilder with blonde hair, green eyes and had the most handsome legs in all of America. Roger was well known for his statuesque physique.

Roger was well known. He and Derek, also a football player, always annoyed me in homeroom. I sat in front of Roger and he would always whisper something annoying in my ear and tease at the way I talked. He would always call me a white girl stuck in a black girl's body and to add insult to injury, he would say that's how I acted. It drove me insane!

One of my biggest pet peeves was someone questioning my *sistah* status. I am extremely proud to be a voluptuous black woman and hated being called anything outside of that. So, at that time in my life both gentlemen were super agitating. I never thought that I would date either one of them.

Yet still, I smiled.

Throw me
to the wolves
and I will return
leading the pack

# Chapter Twelve

One month left to go until school was over for the summer. I had just made the cheerleading squad! My score was the fourth highest, and I was ecstatic. I beat out some of the girls who had been cheering for years. My friends were so excited for me, and it was such a boost to my confidence! So, at the end of the year the new squad cheers for the exhibition games of the new football team.

On game days, we wore our cheerleading uniforms around the school to show our team spirit. Also, the senior week activities took place because the seniors were getting ready to graduate at the end of the year. I remember the day that I walked into my homeroom class with my cheerleading uniform on. This was the day that I realized Roger was attracted to me. I walked in as usual and sat down in my chair in front of him but instead of the annoying banter, he leaned over and whispered into my ear, "I am so proud of you. I knew you were going to do it!" I thought that was so sweet of him. Derek chimed in congratulating me and complimenting me on my try out. However, Roger seemed more serious on that day.

We only spent 15 minutes in homeroom and right towards the end of class before the bell rang to dismiss us, he whispered into my ear.

"You look so beautiful," I blushed. What the heck was wrong with me??!! I had sworn off guys period. I refused to be misled by anymore boys…ever! But the way he said it was so endearing. As he got ready to leave upon the bell ringing, he slowly put his arm around my waist and gently kissed my neck telling me to have a wonderful day. I felt that little kiss tingle from the top of my head to the bottom soles of my feet. All I could think was, *he is hot*!

I needed a distraction. It was the end of the day, and I was getting ready for cheerleading practice out on the field. As I was coming out from the locker room, I saw Mitchell sitting in his red car with Katrina. Katrina, who had a bad reputation at our school for being promiscuous was 19 and already had two sons with two baby daddies. Not to mention she also lived in the projects.

Although she had her reputation, I always felt compassion for her. I knew what it felt like to be humiliated by a sexual reputation. So, I never judged her.

She was a senior and was also graduating along with Mitchell and was also in our law studies class. Katrina was a light-skinned, petite and attractive black girl. She wore her hair in a short-cropped haircut like a hip-hop rapper girl and had a gold tooth. She always wore either very tight jeans or very short skirts. What in the world was she doing in the car with Mitchell? He was racist or, so I assumed. But from the looks of things, they seemed very cozy sitting together in his car. Then something hit me. I was becoming…jealous. What the heck was going on with me? I could not stand this guy yet why was it bothering me to see him with Katrina? So, I quickly dismissed it.

Yet still, I smiled.

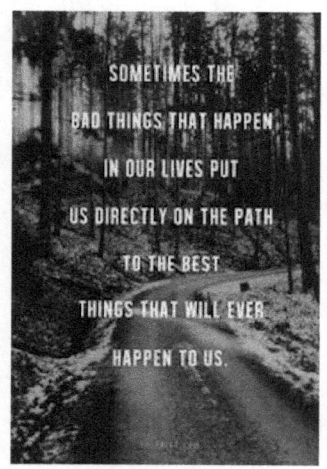

# Chapter Thirteen

Two weeks before the last day of school. Senior week was filled with lots of activities and fun including senior skip day. Everyone skips school on senior skip day and heads to the beach. I was terrified. My mother would have a fit if I ever missed school. In all the years, I attended school I had perfect attendance. I think I only missed one day of school in a six-year period. Of course, my friends were adamant I needed to skip with everybody else. That day as I went to my homeroom, Roger was waiting for me. He asked if I had plans to skip and of course, I told him of my fears. He convinced me to come to the beach and meet him there later in the afternoon. Although I was very hesitant, I decided to get with my best friends and ride down to the beach. If I was going to get in trouble, I might as well make it worth my while!!

We put on our Daisy Dukes and bathing suit tops, and we headed down to the beach. Everyone was there partying hard, sun tanning, playing volleyball and listening to music. It was the perfect environment for skipping. My two best friends and I were just laughing and enjoying ourselves even though I was still nervous. As we were walking down the beach, I ran into Roger. He was so fine. He was shirtless and had on these tight jean shorts with that perfect muscular body looking like the Terminator with another guy friend of his named Jesse. He had the biggest smile on his face when he saw me, and it made me blush! We laughed, talked and played volleyball. We had a great day full of good clean fun. It felt so good to be free.

This year of my life was totally different than the nightmare from the year before. As the day ended, Roger asked if I needed a ride home. I told him I did not need a ride. He asked if he could come and visit me. I gave him my address, but we did not confirm a date or time that he would come to visit. I left the beach with my girlfriends after realizing we were going to get away with skipping. I was able to go home in peace. The day was exciting and anxious at the same time.

Yet still, I smiled.

> In between goals
> is a thing called life,
> that has to be lived
> and enjoyed.
> -Sid Caesar

# Chapter Fourteen

It was the last day of school for the seniors! It was a day to say goodbye. Most of the other students came on this day and skipped the remaining two days of the year. But my mom was not having it. So, of course, I was in attendance. It was a really fun day for us all!

This was the day juniors prepared for being the senior rulers next year, and everybody made it a point to say goodbye with hugs, reminiscing and the signing of the yearbooks.

This was the last day of the year you were going to see the seniors. This was significant for me because two of my classes were senior classes. This day was also very significant for me as far as the guys in my life. Well, guy. When I went to home room on this particular day, Roger was there but had a very serious look on his face. The strangest feeling came over me and I wasn't quite sure why. We said hello like we normally did, but he told me he had something to tell me. He told me that he had just received a full scholarship to a private high school to finish out his high school career because of his amazing stats as a football player.

In other words, he would no longer be attending our school next year. I immediately felt an overwhelming feeling of sadness. I was happy for him, but at the same time, I realized how much I was beginning to have feelings for him. Truth be told, I did not want to see him leave. The school was far away from us, and at that very moment, I knew I would probably never see him again. He had gotten to me, and I didn't even realize it.

In that instance, I wanted us to be more than just friends and now I wasn't going to have the opportunity to be his girlfriend. I was very proud of him for being exemplary at football and his academics all at the same time, although in my heart I was screaming for him to stay.

Please stay! Don't leave me!

My response seemed to put him at ease, and we spent the remaining ten minutes of homeroom class just hugging each other without uttering a single word. We finally broke the silence and let each other know how deeply we felt for one another.

How would I get through the rest of this day? My heart began doing somersaults diving off the cliff in sadness.

It took all the strength left in me to continue throughout the rest of my day. Even with the painful realization of Roger's fate, I did enjoy saying goodbye to all the seniors I knew in each of my classes.

The day was almost over, and I had one more class left which was my Law studies class. It was also the class I shared with Mitchell *'the racist.'* Or was he? After seeing him with Katrina, I was not so sure who he really was. Maybe I had misjudged him the entire time? He came up to me toward the end of our class as everyone was signing each other's yearbook and asked me to sign his. He told me that he was happy for me making the cheerleading squad and enjoyed having me in the class even if all we did was debate with one another. That made me laugh. As he was talking to me, there was a kindness in his eyes that I had never seen before. It was at that very moment, I knew I had misjudged him.

So, I wrote what was in my heart and it went like this:

*A lot of times you come across people that you think are a certain way and they turn out to be different from what you expected. Thank you for a year of challenging me and the great debates we had in each class. I have learned so much. I know you will be very successful in life. Enjoy your summer. If you ever need some advice call me.*

I wrote my phone number. I wrote that as a joke. I never would expect him to ever call me. He read my note right there in front of me and looked at me in the most endearing way and gave me a hug goodbye. I do not know what came over me but at that very moment I felt sad, and I was going to miss him. This was just an extremely emotional day full of confusing feelings.

Why was I so devastated about Roger? We never kissed or dated or anything. Yet, I felt like I had lost my boyfriend. And why did I even think twice about Mitchell? I never liked him anyway! But I felt so sad that the following day when I would arrive to class, he would no longer be there. This was sheer confusion for me.

Yet still, I smiled.

*Even after tragedy, if you choose to live, you will find a new purpose and way to enjoy your life!!!*

— A. Fox

# Chapter Fifteen

Summer had officially started and proved to be the summer that changed my life. This summer I really had no plans other than to work. I had no social life, so I would just come home and watch TV. This seemed to be my plan for the entire summer until I received contact from someone that changed that plan significantly.

One day I was sitting at home and I received a phone call. The guy on the phone seemed to be very nice and said that he was just calling to say hello to me. As he began to ask me questions I really did not know who he was. He continued to describe himself and even describe the classes we had together, but for the life of me I just drew a blank and did not know who he was. Finally, it hit me! It was Mitchell!!! He said I had written my phone number in his yearbook and he thought why not give me a call. I forgot that I had given him my phone number. I was so embarrassed and felt like I had made him feel like he was insignificant. But he did not take it that way at all.

We talked for four hours that day nonstop. He was kind and funny. And we had a lot in common. It was so natural speaking with him. How could I have missed judged such an amazing guy? I remember not wanting to get off the phone with him the first day. But in the following weeks it began to become the norm.

We talked every day for hours. You would have thought to yourself, *how much would they have to talk about?* But it never seemed that way. It seemed like we never had enough time to talk. I really began to like him… a lot. About three weeks had passed and Mitchell and I spoken every day. I remember one day I was sitting in my room after we had just finished having another two to three-hour conversation. My mom comes into my room and says there is a gentleman at the door for me. Well, her exact words were,

"Who is this white boy at my front door for you?"

I had no idea who she was speaking of. I'd been talking to Mitchell for the past three weeks, but he did not know where I lived. He would never just *pop up* at my house. I was just as curious as to who she was talking about and who it could be.

So, I got up to go to the door to see who it was. And to my total surprise there was a handsome, blonde, buff beau with the most perfect physique of a man I had ever witnessed standing before me with two bouquets of red roses. It was Roger! I was in a state of shock to say the least. It took me a moment to get my bearings together and my words in order to ask what he was doing at my house?

My mom was extremely strict and all I could think was, I'm about to go down once again with the Titanic! Instead he said in the politest manner,

"Ma'am I am so sorry to come by unannounced, but I did not have your daughters phone number only her address and I had to see her. I wanted to give the mother of this beautiful young woman some flowers and hope that you would give me the opportunity to speak with her."

He had my mom at '*Ma'am*'. He was so charming, that she let him in and had him meet my little brother. She told him it was ok to see me. I was floored, smiling from ear to ear and I could not stop blushing. To say I was happy to see him would've been an understatement. We talked that entire evening and did not go anywhere! We just sat at my apartment complex outside and just got to know each other better than we ever did in home room. Roger was amazing, smart and goal oriented. Most of all, completely gorgeous.

Everything a woman would want when dating a man. But the reality was he lived so far away, and our time together would still be short-lived. And that always stayed in the back of my mind.

That night before he walked me to my door, he kissed me for the first time. I felt that kiss in my knees. It was gentle and sensual unlike anybody else I had ever kissed. We said goodbye without me even knowing if I would ever see him again. It was one of the best days I ever had.

Then a ball of confusion had begun to set in. The two guys that I never would have ever thought I would like are the two men that I like the most now. Life really knows how to throw those curveballs, right?

Yet still, I smiled.

> "If you're brave enough to say goodbye, life will reward you with a new hello."
>
> – *Paulo Coelho*

# Chapter Sixteen

Two more weeks went by and my encounter with Roger was just that, an encounter. I have not heard from him since that time but continued to talk to Mitchell every day. Mitchell was beginning to become the staple in my life. We talked every day on schedule and still for hours. My mom would even answer the phone sometimes and begin having conversations with him. She liked him a lot. He was very smart, almost like a genius so he would give her advice once she decided to return to college in her 40's. At this point he was a true friend.

Then one day I was home alone, and I heard a knock at the door. It was Roger again! He said he had been away practicing at football camp and that is why I hadn't heard from him. We sat and talked for hours.

As our conversation was ending, we finally decided to define our relationship. The reality was we would not have the time to enjoy each other or spend time with one another for it to grow into anything because of the distance between us. What we knew was that we had the potential for a great relationship, but in life, timing is everything. If your timing is off, then it just will not work. But timing for enjoying each other at that very moment was right. And we decided to enjoy each other completely at least one time in our life.

With both of us understanding that this would probably be our only time together we took full advantage of it. After the traumatic incident with what happened to me I never thought I would ever want to feel the touch of another man against my skin again. But the deep feelings I had for him and the feelings he had for me made me very comfortable. The moment for us could not be any more perfect than it was at that moment.

He was gentle and sensual to me. We were together and ended with a cuddle, forehead kiss and conversation.

Intimacy makes a big difference. He drew me close and kissed me as if he never wanted to let me go. He never had to tell me he loved me because I felt it. I loved him too and we cherished this one moment we had together, knowing in our heart of hearts that we would never see each other again. It's a moment we would always have that we will cherish and remember for the rest of our lives. It will forever stay tucked away in our hearts.

I watched him walk off into the sunset and when I closed the door, I cried, and I cried. That chapter of my life with him was now closed.

Yet still, I smiled.

# Chapter Seventeen

In life, when one chapter closes another one opens. A week had passed since my amazing, yet sad encounter with Roger. But Mitchell and I continued to get closer and closer. Eventually, he finally decided to ask me out on a real date. At this point, we were at the midpoint of summer.

He had never been to my house, so it was going to be the first time we ever went out on a date. It was also the first time that he would be meeting my family in person. I was looking forward to our first date and he wanted to take me out to dinner and have a nice walk on the beach afterward. My favorite place in the entire world is the beach. The ocean is huge, and the waves come rushing in every day on shore. The reason I think I love the ocean so much is because for so long in my life I just wanted to run away and escape. I wanted to swim out to the sea of the unknown and drift where ever the water would take me. I would imagine the islands being so beautiful and peaceful that it became my ultimate bliss in life. The waves would come in and represent the turbulence that sometimes happens in our lives. Another Reason I love the ocean is because even though the waves come in and stop at the shore, it's a reminder that eventually, whatever you are going through in life (the waves) will end. And when the waves are gone you have the opportunity once again to swim back out to the beautiful ocean.

My mom began to set a curfew for dating and was now allowing me to do so. I wanted to look especially nice for Mitchell, so I chose a mini dress and did my make up to look especially pretty. Mitchell was a very handsome man, 6'3" blonde and beautiful chameleon eyes. I had not seen him since the last day of school, so I was excited to see him again. My mom answered the door when he arrived, and she was so excited! She ran to the back to tell me there was a handsome young and very, very polite young man at the door. My little brother liked him as well. He spent time to get to know him, and I thought that was very nice. When I came in the room, his eyes lit up, so I knew he liked what he saw. It made me feel like the effort I put into looking nice paid off. He came and hugged me, and we had a brief conversation at that moment with my entire family, and then we were off.

For our first date, he took me to my favorite seafood restaurant, and we enjoyed a delicious platter for two. The conversation was nice, and we held hands and walked together which was extremely comforting. We did get a lot of stares, and my apprehension was up because he was white, and I was black. So to put me at ease he teased me by stating they were not looking at us because we were a mixed couple, they were looking because he was so tall and I was so short, 4'11" at the time!

At any rate, once people saw us interact and how genuine we were with one another it would surely put a smile on their faces. After dinner, we drove down to the beach and parked directly in front. It was so magical, and I am a sucker for romance!

It was the perfect ending to an absolutely wonderful dinner. We laughed and talked again for a couple of hours and then he reached over and kissed me for the first time. It was magical. At that time in my life, if perfection was real, we were it.

He was everything I wanted in a man. I believed I had found my soul mate. He took me home, kissed me again and got me home in plenty of time before my curfew. My mom loved that. And when he called me that night to tell me he had made it home I knew I was going to fall in love with him. And I did with all my heart.

Our summer together proved to be an epic teenage romance like you see in the movies. I was with him every day of my life, and he was the only guy who knew everybody in my family from my mother's side of the family to my father's side, and I did not even grow up with my dad. He knew my aunts, uncles, and cousins. He would go with me everywhere. Whether it was the bad side of town or the good side of town. Whether it was the beach, his pizza shop, or my house, we fell madly in love. The more we were together, the more in love we became.

The tragedy that I had experienced just a year prior seemed almost invisible. I was happier than I had ever been in my life! All anyone ever wants in this world is to be loved, and I found the perfect love for me.

What I have learned in life is to celebrate the wins yet prepare for the challenges. I also have realized that life is a constant opportunity to overcome. No matter what the situation is, you have the ability and the strength to continue moving in life. Your tragedy does not have to define who you are. Your courage and belief that you can overcome anything is what defines you. Was this time one of the happiest times in my life?

## The Pain Behind The Smile

Yes, it was, however, it also prepared me for the tragedies to come.

Yet still, I smiled.

### The End

# About the Author

"Promoting positive reinforcement and true change in our community through the purest form of communication there is."

Angela Foxworth currently resides in Marietta, Ga with her husband and has two adult children and her first born grandson. She has always had the desire to use her love of journalism and people to become a multi-faceted global talk show host. Her passion to reach the masses is the reason she became an author. With the support of her family, friends and business partners, Angela Foxworth has now become an international talk show host, celebrity red carpet host and is the reigning Mrs. Georgia Woman US majesty 2020. She is positioning herself to use her platform for the purpose of educating, motivating and inspiring people all over the world. She believes that coming together and finding common ground is the most effective way to build lasting relationships.

She hopes as a Best-Selling author that her books will inspire people to overcome the most difficult odds and to have determination within themselves. No matter what happens in life you will always find a way to accomplish your dreams.

Life with A Fox is living outside the box and she wants everyone she comes in contact to experience just that!

Angela Foxworth aka "A Fox"

Talk Show Host on XOD tv and founder of The Angela Foxworth Show

Instagram: @afoxradio and therealafox

Twitter: @foxworth_angela

Email: info@theafoxshow.com

Website: Talk Show Host | "The Angela Foxworth Show"

Talk Show Host | "The Angela Foxworth Show"

Talk Show Host Angela Foxworth Is Interviewing With A Purpose Through Facebook Live, Blogtalk Radio and Xperien On Demand. Tune In Every Monday "The Angela Foxworth Show" For Hot Topics!

Facebook: Angela Collins-Foxworth and Angela Foxworth

www.ingramcontent.com/pod-product-compliance
Lightning Source LLC
Chambersburg PA
CBHW071121160426
**43196CB00013B/2661**